The Investment Puzzle: Risk and Reward

By Roger Sies

The Investment Puzzle: Risk and Reward

By Roger Sies

The Investment Puzzle: Risk and Reward

Copyright © 2021 by Roger Sies. All rights reserved.

Published by Enterprise Publishing

Limit of Liability/Disclaimer of Warranty:
While the publisher and author have used the utmost of care in preparing this book, they make no representations or warranties with regard to the completeness or accuracy of the contents of this book, and disclaim any implied warranties of merchantability or fitness for a specific purpose. No warranty may be created or extended by sales materials or sales representatives. The author and publisher are <u>not</u> engaged in rendering investment advice and are <u>not</u> providing investment advice or recommending any investment strategies. The information and example strategies discussed in this book may not be suitable for your situation, and you should consult a professional when appropriate. Neither the author nor the publisher shall be liable for any financial loss or for any other commercial or personal damages, including but not limited to special, incidental, consequential, or other damages.

Dedicated to my wife, Andrea Ann Wargo, Ph.D, who has been my partner in all aspects of my life, including investing. She helps me to clarify my thinking, and she is supportive in all my endeavors. She also spends her precious time editing my writing. Without her help, this book would not have been written.

Table of Contents

PREFACE

Which is the more important question, "How do I get the highest return on my investments?" or "How much return do I need to achieve my goals?" So, "How much investment risk do I need to take?" This is the investment puzzle.

I once had a colleague who, about once a month, thought of a new way to beat the market and become rich. At first it seemed that each ploy was working, but in the end each failed, and he was no better off than when he started. He brought many friends and colleagues into his plans, and they all lost money. They also wasted time and lost the opportunity to improve their financial position. He wanted to make a killing to get rich quick instead of patiently investing in companies he had researched and found financially solid and successful over the years.

Once an investor has an established portfolio it is fine to take a "flier" on an investment that does not have an established track record. This type of investment should make up a very small portion of a portfolio. Remember that the companies which are solid and established today are not necessarily the same companies as those ten or more years ago. Things change. Portfolios sometimes need change, but good investing habits do not change. Patience, research and thought before either buying or selling are time-tested virtues.

This book shows how different investments grow at various rates of return over various time periods. It also tells how to research risk levels and other factors such as tax implications, portfolio turnover, and investment costs. This book is not intended to tell you how to invest, but instead, describes different approaches so you can decide which is the best approach for you.

Tables 18 and 19, on pages 75 and 76, demonstrate how effective it is to save and invest as early as possible.

INTRODUCTION

The premise of this book is that you, as an investor, should take only as much risk as necessary to reach your goals. This seems sensible and easy, but, as usual, "The devil is in the details." Ask yourself:

- How much money do I already have invested?
- How much can I afford to invest periodically?
- How much money do I want or need at retirement?
- How long until I retire?
- What average rate of return will I need?

Once you have the answers to the first four questions, insert your data into a table similar to Table 1 below. Your own data can be used with *Time Value of Money* calculations to help answer the last question. (See Time Value of Money page 45.)

Table 1. Average Rate of Return Needed

	Already Invested	Periodic Investment	Amount Needed	Years Until Retirement	Average Rate of Return
	-$25,000	-$6,000	$2,000,000	45	6.65%
Pages/ Numbers	present-value	payment	future-value	num-periods	Rate function
Excel	PV	Pmt	FV	Nper	Rate function

Table 1 demonstrates a hypothetical 20 year old investor, with $25,000 in savings, who invests $6,000 a year for 45 years with an average rate of return of 6.65% (after investment expenses, taxes and inflation), achieves the goal of $2,000,000 for retirement. Plug in your numbers to get your answer.

This Table shows the connection between your goals and the amount of risk you need to achieve them. If your goals require more or less than $2,000,000, your rate of return will need to be adjusted with a commensurate level of risk. If you are not comfortable with the rate of return needed, you will need to adjust your goals or parameters. This calculation only serves as a rough estimate.

Table 1 was produced with *Apple Pages* using the *Rate* function. *Apple Numbers* works exactly the same as *Apple Pages*. *Excel* can provide the same information, but uses slightly different terminology. The function in *Pages*, *Numbers*, and *Excel* used to determine the needed rate of return is called *Rate*. The data needed are the same. Rows 3 and 4 of Table 1 show the terminology used by *Pages*, *Numbers* and *Excel*. To produce Table 1 the first four values are needed. The *Rate* Function solves and fills in the needed rate of return.

Goals must be formulated by the investor and must:

• be quantifiable and realistic;

• form a target dollar amount needed for investment;

• form a target amount for the desired portfolio value at the time of retirement.

To determine the needed rate of return, investment costs, taxes and inflation must be included in your average rate calculations. The investor must also have knowledge of income and expenses to know how much can be invested.

Personal financial software can aid the investor to answer the questions of how much money one has, and how much of that money he or she can afford to invest. See *Budgeting Made Easier* later in this book.

Elements of Risk and Reward, investment costs, taxes and inflation, and the *Time Value of Money* calculation are discussed in the book.

CREATE A BUDGET

Before you start to invest you need to have some savings as a cushion. Saving is simple; spend less than you earn! Although this is simple, it is not easy. A budget is helpful to find where you can cut expenses and save. When creating a budget, keep a list of your expenditures for a short period of time. Use the list to identify categories for the budget. See the four steps below for creating a budget.

Step 1 - Keep a list of expenses and income (Sample list below)

- 1/2/2021 Groceries Acme Market -$42.95

- 1/2/2021 Medical Aspirin Acme Drug -$12.98

- 1/4/2021 Insurance First Insurance -$248.55

- 1/6/2021 Personal Care Haircut Bill's Barber Shop - $30.00

- 1/28/2021 Salary Acme Inc. $1,200.00

- 1/31/2021 Groceries Acme Market -$23.49

Step 2 - Gather the data needed

- Expenses

  - The list of expenses you compiled in Step 1

  - Receipts for cash expenditures

  - Checking account statements

  - Credit Card statements

  - Rent, mortgage, loan (such as auto loan) statements

  - Utility bills

  - Tax Returns

- Income

  - 1099s

  - Checking account statements

- Bank account statements

- Brokerage statements

Step 3 - Categorize the data

After you have reviewed the data collected in Step 2, you can see how your expenses fit into categories. Your list should be detailed enough for you to determine what categories you will need in your budget. Arranging expenses in categories will help you determine where you can cut your expenses, if needed. The following is a partial list of your likely expense categories.

- Insurance

- Groceries

- Personal Care

- Automotive

- Federal Income Tax

- State Income Tax

- Utilities

- Medical

- Eating Out

- Recreation

- Charity

- Gifts

Organizing your expenses into categories is the best way to see how you are actually spending your money. The next step is to divide the categories into non-discretionary and discretionary expenses. Non-discretionary expenses are those expenses that are necessary for you to live. They are also the expenses you will need to cover in retirement.

Some examples of non-discretionary expenses are:

- Taxes

- Utility bills

- Mortgage payments

- Credit card payments

- Insurance payments

- Health care

- Rent

- Debt repayment

- Auto fuel and repair

- Groceries

Discretionary expenses are the expenses you are able to reduce or eliminate in order to save more money.

Some examples of discretionary spending are:

- Hobbies
- Non-business travel
- Restaurants
- Entertainment such as movies, and shows
- Alcohol and smoking

Step 4 - Set up your budget

Your budget can be one of several types. It can be completely manual using a columnar pad and pencil, a self designed spreadsheet, or a pre-designed commercial software package. You need to set up your budget so that you will be able to know how much you spend in each category each month, and at the end of each year. Total the expenses for each month and compare the total to your total income. If the expenses are higher than income, look for categories where you can make cuts.

When you receive a raise, pretend you didn't get it, and save the extra money. A well set up budget that is kept up to date is very useful in several ways. You will be better able to determine where you can save more money, and you will know where you stand both in accumulating assets and meeting your goals. The steps outlined above are necessary to set up any type of budget. You need only to do the budget setup process once, although you may need to update it from time to time. Maintaining the budget is different; you need to do this every day. This can be monotonous, difficult and very time consuming, but rewarding.

Reliable financial information is essential to reach your goals. Read the next section to see how to get these data without as much effort on your part.

Your goal is to spend less than you earn, <u>save and invest</u> the remainder, and have good reliable financial data at your finger tips when you need it.

How Will Expenses Change In Retirement?

Start with your current expenses which you should know from the budget you keep. Make adjustments for those expenses that increase, decrease, or go away. The following are examples of expenses that are likely to change:

• Housing can either decrease or increase. You may decide to downsize your home or to move to a more expensive location;

• Employment related expenses such as parking, clothing, and education may decrease;

• Second cars and related expenses may go away;

• Social Security and pension plan expenses will disappear;

• Taxes can go either way, depending on the changes to your income, your IRAs, and the potential changes to tax rates;

- Health care expenses will most likely increase. This could be a large increase;

- Travel and recreation expenses will most likely increase during early retirement and then decrease later.

These are just examples, and will not apply to all. For example, you may decide to take a part time job for added income or for social interaction. The further you are from retirement, the more difficult it will be to make estimates of your retirement expenses, but the effort is worthwhile.

BUDGETING MADE EASIER

Keeping a full budget manually, or with a spreadsheet, is time consuming and a luxury few busy adults can afford. Today, inexpensive, even free, computer programs can do the job for you. In most cases, you do not even need to enter data. *Personal Capital* (free) and *Quicken* (inexpensive) are two of these programs. Both of these programs draw the data needed from your credit cards and checking accounts for expenses, and from your brokerage accounts and banking accounts for income. Both programs require a quick and easy set up for expense and income accounts, linking them to your credit cards, banks and brokerage accounts. The only other thing you need to do is to pay most of your expenses from credit cards or from your checking account, and have your salary automatically deposited into your bank account. Once this set up is complete, you may occasionally need to add some details to clarify the expenditure. You then not only have a complete accounting of your expenses and income, but also an accounting of all your financial assets.

You instantly know your financial position. The software packages keep track of all your brokerage accounts, credit card accounts and bank accounts. They provide portfolio performance reports and asset allocation reports. They also provide a complete listing of all credit card and checking transactions. These programs are helpful at tax time because they provide a listing of your income and expenses in one place.

Note: If you use credit cards, try to pay them off at the end of each month. Interest payments on your credit cards are a roadblock to saving money.

WHAT YOU NEED TO KNOW ABOUT RISK AND REWARD

In investing there is a well known relationship between risk and reward. The riskier the investment, the higher the reward. However, the riskier the investment, the more likely it is to fail, and the more likely you are to lose money.

While acquiring investments, you must have an understanding of how your money grows over time with various levels of risk and return.

You must also have a firm view of your goals and adjust them over time as circumstances change. Goals help determine how much investment risk you need to take.

Types of Investment Risk

Investment risk is normally classified as either Systematic or Nonsystematic. Systematic risk cannot be diversified while Nonsystematic risk can be diversified.

Systematic Risk is the risk of volatility of the market as a whole and the uncertainty in the economy.

Examples of systematic risk are:

- <u>Market Risk</u>; security price fluctuations
- <u>Interest Rate Risk</u>; changes in interest rates.
- <u>Reinvestment Rate Risk</u>; the risk that the reinvestment rate will be lower than that of the original investment.
- <u>Purchasing Power Risk</u> or Inflation.
- <u>Exchange Rate Risk</u>; foreign currency fluctuations.

Nonsystematic Risk is the risk inherent in the business itself, including:

- <u>Business Risk</u>; the risk the business will not be efficient, have legal problems, or not produce a product or service that is salable.
- <u>Financial Risk</u>; the risk that the firm's sources of financing will not prove adequate.

How to gauge the risk of an investment

A good way to measure the risk of any one investment is its *Beta* which measures the volatility of the stock or fund relative to the Market. *Beta* measures the expected price move of a stock or fund relative to the movement of the stock market as a whole.

If the *Beta* of a stock is 1, the stock's price, on average, goes up or down the same amount as the whole stock market. If the market goes up 10%, the stock goes up 10%. If the *Beta* is 1.5 and the market goes up 10%, the stock goes up 15%. However, if the market goes down 10%, the stock goes <u>down</u> 15%.

Many brokerage house websites such as Fidelity and Schwab and independent websites such as Zacks have research capabilities that give the *Beta* and other information about stocks and funds. *Edgar* on the *Securities and Exchange Commission* website (<u>sec.gov</u>) is also a good resource. Do as much research as possible on various websites about potential investments.

Remember that all investments have risk, some more that others. There are strategies to mitigate risk, but there are no strategies to eliminate it. <u>Not investing</u> is also a risk.

ASSET ALLOCATION AND DIVERSIFICATION

Every savvy investor becomes familiar with the nonsystematic risks listed above, and knows the value of asset allocation and diversification.

Asset allocation is spreading investments among different asset classes such as stocks, index funds, mutual funds, exchange traded funds, bonds, cash and cash equivalents. Diversification is spreading investments further within different asset classes, such as sectors like utilities and retail, and among different companies. To see how various asset allocations have been rewarded over the past 45 years see Tables 14 through 17, beginning on page 69.

Different ways to achieve diversification include picking securities from different companies within these various categories or investing in index funds or mutual funds.

When starting to invest, it is probably better to invest in index funds or in mutual funds, since mutual funds hold a variety of companies, and index funds can hold the whole market to provide diversification.

A good investment strategy is to build your portfolio through dollar cost averaging. To dollar cost average, arrange with a fund or brokerage firm to buy a specified dollar amount of an asset at the current price periodically, usually monthly or quarterly. If the price of the asset is lower you buy more shares, if higher, you buy fewer shares. Dollar cost averaging takes the emotion out of investing by investing the same amount in an asset regularly.

GOALS AND RISK

Goals help determine the amount of assets needed during a lifetime, and the need for assets helps determine the amount of risk to take while investing. Goals may change over the course of a person's life. In the early stages of life while people are getting established in a career, financial goals probably include paying off debt and saving some money. At this point the extra money is usually put into a savings or a checking account. A little later, investing will probably be in a money market account and then in an index fund or in a mutual fund. Individual stocks that you have carefully researched and believe will perform well could be gradually and carefully added. Eventually, the goal turns to retirement. Now the investor could shift the portfolio to include more fixed assets. These assets could be in the form or either cash (money market funds) or bonds. Care must be taken not to become conservative to the point of eliminating growth from the portfolio. Growth is essential to reach your goals.

There will be other goals which are of a more personal nature. These goals include buying a home, children's education, and automobiles.

All goals must be considered when determining how much return you need from your investments, and how much risk you need to take. These decisions involve considerable thought. Budgets are important and helpful, but you may still consider using an expert to help with your financial planning. If you consult an expert investment advisor, make sure that advisor meets the fiduciary standard and is legally bound to act in your best interest. Beware of the advisor who is just a salesperson.

BALANCING RISK AND REWARD

There is a balancing act between risk and reward. Too little risk and you run out of money before reaching your goals; too much risk and you lose the money you have worked for and saved. The key is to be able to make a reasonably good estimate of how much money you will need at the time of retirement. The further you are away from retirement, the harder this estimate will be. You need to be cognizant of your finances. How much do you spend on average each month? What out of the ordinary expenses are you likely to encounter, such as large purchases, trips, health care? The trick is to take only as much risk as you need to reach your goals. You do need to have a cushion in case you have underestimated your needs or overstated the return on your investments. It is wise to update your estimate at least once each year.

How Investments Provide a Reward

The value of an investment can increase over time (capital gains), and the investment can pay dividends or interest. Dividends can be received either as cash and used for any purpose, or the dividends can be reinvested. A dividend reinvestment is received as an increase in the number of shares of the investment.

Bonds pay a set rate of interest. The reward for investing in bonds is the set interest rate they earn and the promise of the return of principal at maturity. They may also offer favorable tax benefits.

Before counting your rewards be sure you have taken into account your investment costs, taxes and inflation.

INVESTMENT OPTIONS

The most common assets found in the portfolios of investors are index funds, mutual funds, stocks, bonds, cash and cash equivalents.

Index Funds

Index Funds are ideal for starting your portfolio. A whole market index or an S&P 500 index provides excellent diversification. Also, Index fund expenses are low. They also tend to be tax efficient. Portfolio turnover rates are low, therefore, capital gains will be lower which means lower tax expense. Note, as we will see later, returns on stocks, on average, have been higher than returns on bonds.

Mutual Funds

Mutual Funds are also good for acquiring adequate diversification in your portfolio. They tend to have higher costs than index funds and a higher portfolio turnover ratio which equates to higher tax costs.

Returns of mutual funds depend on the individual fund managers since they are responsible for deciding which companies to include in the funds. This means that actively managed mutual funds must have higher returns than index funds to produce the same net monetary gain.

Individual Stocks and Bonds

If you already hold enough index or mutual funds for adequate diversification, then individual stocks and bonds could make sense. The only fees, if any, would be brokerage fees, and you would control turnover. You also decide which companies' stocks or bonds to buy.

Alternative Investments

Although alternative investments are not covered in this book, it is good to be aware of them. Alternative investments include:

- Real estate and Real Estate Investment Trusts (REITS);

- Hedge funds;

- Private equity funds;

- Venture capital;

- Commodities;

- Futures;

- Derivatives contracts;

- Art and Digital Art;

- Antiques;

- Gold, Silver and other precious medals;

- Cryptocurrency.

These investments tend to be less liquid than the investments we have discussed. Most of these investments are <u>not</u> regulated by the SEC. Do your due diligence in researching these investments, and be sure that you understand them <u>before</u> you invest.

International Investments

Investing in international stocks or bonds increases diversification. Many international companies do not follow the same accounting standards as companies in the United States. Because of either different accounting standards or the lack of accounting standards, researching and comparing international companies to U. S. companies is difficult and many times impossible. There is also currency exchange risk, political risk and taxation issues involved with international investments.

Consider the risks and the rewards involved in international investing carefully before investing. Investment advisors have a wide range of recommendations for the allocation of international investments in a portfolio. Seek assistance from your investment professional about the allocation that is reasonable for you.

Cryptocurrencies

Cryptocurrency is one of the best examples I can give for the relationship of risk and reward. You can either make a lot of money or lose everything investing in cryptocurrency. Two ways to invest in cryptocurrency are:

- Buy and sell the cryptocurrencies;
- Buy stock in companies that deal in some way with cryptocurrency.

Problems with investing in cryptocurrency include:

- High volatility

- Lack of current regulation

- Vulnerability to hacking

- Safe storage

- Vulnerable to criminal activity such as money laundering and tax evasion.

If you decide to invest in cryptocurrency **do your research and make sure you understand how cryptocurrency works before you invest.**

INVESTMENT EXPENSES

Paying too much in investment costs can be as devastating as a steep downturn in the market. Too high investment cost may not be as dramatic a loss, but it is a long term loss that can be unnoticed but very costly over the years. Also, be aware of annuity costs, brokerage fees, fund fees, and investment advisor fees. Some of the types of fees involved with investing are as follows:

- 12B-1 fee or marketing costs;
- Purchase and redemption fees;
- Front end load, a fee charged to buy shares;
- Back end load, a fee charged to sell shares;
- Commissions, fees to brokers for various services;
- Custodian fees usually for fulfilling IRS reporting regulations for IRAs;
- Cost of the spread. This is the spread between the bid and the ask price of the security. The investor pays the ask price but receives only the bid price when the security is sold.

Annuity Costs

- Commissions - payment to a salesperson for selling you the annuity
- Underwriting - fees to those who take actuarial risk on benefits (Actuarial risk is the risk that the assumptions used in the annuity may prove to be inaccurate.)
- Fund Management - most annuities invest in mutual funds and the fees are passed to the investor in the annuity.
- Penalties - In most cases, both the annuity issuer and the IRS charge early withdrawal penalties.

Be very careful to read and understand the annuity contract, including the fine print. **Never invest in something you do not understand.** If necessary, consult a professional who has no personal or financial interest in the investment.

Taxes are also a Cost of Investing

How are Investments taxed?

<u>Dividends</u>

Internal Revenue Service (IRS) Topic No. 404 Dividends (Updated 12-Mar-2021) says: "Dividends are the most common type of distribution from a corporation. They're paid out of the earnings and profits of the corporation. Dividends can be classified either as ordinary or qualified. Whereas ordinary dividends are taxable as ordinary income, qualified dividends that meet certain requirements are taxed at lower capital gain rates. The payer of the dividend is required to correctly identify each type and amount of dividend for you when reporting them on your form 1099-DIV for tax purposes. For a definition of qualified dividends, refer to Publication 550, Investment Income and Expenses."

<u>Capital Gains</u>

IRS Topic No. 409 Capital Gains and Losses from the IRS (last Reviewed or Updated 12-Mar-2021) says: "Almost everything you own and use for personal or investment purposes is a capital asset. Examples include a home, personal-use items like household furnishings, and stocks or bonds held as investments. When you sell a capital asset, the difference between the adjusted basis in the asset and the amount you realized from the sale is a capital gain or a capital loss. Generally, an asset's basis is its cost to the owner, but if you received the asset as a gift or inheritance refer to <u>Topic No. 703</u> for information about your basis. For Information on calculation for adjusted basis, refer to <u>Publication 551, Basis of Assets</u>. You have a capital gain if you sell the asset for more than your adjusted basis. You have a capital loss if you sell the asset for less than your adjusted basis. Losses from the sale of personal-use property, such as your home or car, aren't tax deductible."

IRS Topic No. 409 then talks about short-term and long-term capital gains or losses: "To correctly arrive at your net capital gain or loss, capital gains and losses are classified as long-term or short-term. Generally, if you hold the asset for more than one year before you dispose of it, your capital gain or loss is long-term. If you hold it one year or less, your capital gain or loss is short-term.

For exceptions to this rule, such as property acquired by gift, property acquired from a decedent, or patent property, refer to IRS <u>Publication 544, Sales and Other Dispositions of Assets</u>; or for commodity futures, see IRS <u>Publication 550, Investment Income and Expenses</u>. To determine how long you held the asset, you generally count from the day after the day you acquired the asset up to and including the day you disposed of the asset.

If you have a net capital gain, a lower tax rate may apply to the gain than the tax rate that applies to your ordinary income. The term 'net capital gain' means the amount by which your net long-term gain for the year is more than your net short-term capital loss for the year. The term 'net long-term capital gain' means long term capital gains reduced by long-term capital losses including any unused long-term capital loss carried over from previous years."

If this isn't complicated enough, we still have not talked about Capital Gains Tax Rates or the limit on the deduction and carryover of losses. These issues and some others are dependent on each investor's specific circumstances. Since the remaining issues are so investor specific and are <u>prone to rapid change</u>, consult your brokerage firm or your tax accountant for answers to your individual investment tax issues. **To mitigate taxes, it is important <u>not</u> to sell capital assets without careful consideration and research.**

Capital Gains within a Mutual Fund

The following is from the *IRS Interactive Tax Assistant - Frequently Asked Questions* (Updated 4-Jan-2021)

"Question
I received a 1099-DIV showing a capital gain. Why do I have to report capital gains from my mutual funds if I never sold any shares of the mutual fund?

Answer
A mutual fund is a regulated investment company that pools funds of investors allowing them to take advantage of a diversity of investments and professional asset management.

You own shares in the mutual fund but the fund owns capital assets, such as stock, corporate bonds, government obligations, etc. One of the ways the fund makes money for you is to sell these assets at a gain.

If the mutual fund held the capital asset for more than one year, the nature of the income is capital gain, and the mutual fund passes it on to you as a capital gain distribution. These capital gain distributions are usually paid to you or credited to your mutual fund account, and are considered income to you. Form 1099-DIV Dividends and Distributions distinguishes capital gain distributions from other types of income, such as ordinary dividends.

Consider capital gain distributions as long-term capital gains no matter how long you've owned shares in the mutual fund."

Investment cost can seem to be trivial but can really add up. The following table demonstrates how investment cost for a $25,000 investment can reduce the value of your investment over 45 years.

Table 2. Investment Cost

	Period	Return Net of Cost	Investment	Investment Value after 45 years
Return before Investment Cost	**45**	10%	-$25,000	$1,822,262
Return after Cost of 0.5%	**45**	9.5%	-$25,000	$1,484,483
Return after Cost of 2%	**45**	8%	-$25,000	$798,011

With cost of just 0.5%, the value of the investment at the end of 45 years is reduced by $337,779, the difference between $1,822,262 and $1,484,483. With cost of 2% the value is reduced by $1,024,251, the difference between $1,822,262 and $798,011.

Research your investments carefully both for quality and for expenses.

For an eye-opening discussion of investment costs and taxes, read *"The Little Book of Common Sense Investing"* by John C. Bogle, published by John Wiley & Sons, Inc., Hoboken, New Jersey in 2007.

TIME VALUE OF MONEY

What tool can help us know how much an investment or the whole portfolio will grow over time? The tool is Future Value, which is included in the concept of the *Time Value of Money*. An example of Future Value (FV) is Compound Interest. If the interest rate is 5%, and the principal is $100, there is $5 interest at the end of the year. The calculation is (100 x .05) = $5. With compound interest, the interest is added to the principal making it $105. The calculation for the second year is $105 + (105 x .05) = $110.25.

Time Value of Money concepts are very important in Finance. These concepts are usually used to evaluate and to compare the financial results of two or more investments. The *Time Value of Money* is divided into four concepts: Present Value, Future Value, the Future Value of an Annuity, and the Present Value of an Annuity. In this book we will use Future Value to show how a portfolio grows with various rates of return and how expenses accumulate over time.

Understanding Simple and Compound Interest will help to understand the Future Value concept.

Table 3. Simple Interest

Period	Interest Rate	Principal	Interest	Balance
Year 1	5%	$1,000.00	$50.00	$1,050.00
Year 2			$50.00	$1,100.00
Year 3			$50.00	$1,150.00

Notice that in the second and third year, interest is only computed on the <u>original principal</u> and not on the balance.

Table 4. Compound Interest

Period	Interest Rate	Principal	Interest	Balance
Year 1	5%	$1,000.00	$50.00	$1,050.00
Year 2			$52.50	$1,102.50
Year 3			$55.13	$1,157.63

With compound interest, the interest is computed on the balance with each year's interest added to the principal.

Table 5. Future Value Calculation

Rate of Return	Initial Investment	Periodic Investment	Number of Periods	Future Value
5%	-$1,000	0	3	$1,157.63

The Future Value of a Single Sum is the future amount that the initial investment grows to when it is compounded for a given number of periods at a given interest rate.

Future Value (FV) can be calculated with a financial calculator or with a computer. *Excel*, *Numbers* or *Pages* are among the software programs that can be used on the computer to perform FV calculations. The calculation in Table 5 was performed in *Pages*. All that needs to be done is to select the Future Value function and to enter the values that are asked for.

Notice the Future Value balance in Table 5 is the same as the balance in Table 4. For a large number of periods, the Future Value Calculation would be more practical and easier, and both calculations would yield the same result. It you needed to change values such as the Interest Rate at some point in the calculation, use the compound interest model in Table 4.

Future Value (FV) Formula

$$FV = I \times (1 + r)^n$$

> Where:
> FV = Future Value
> I =Initial Investment
> r = Rate of Return
> n = Number of Periods

In Table 6 below, where do the data for the FV calculation come from?

- <u>Rate of Return</u> is an estimate over a long period of time and should be a conservative number. See page 54 for historical data.

- <u>Initial Investment</u> is the first investment made for the security.

- <u>Periodic Investment</u>, in this case, is an additional investment to the security each year.

- <u>Number of Periods</u>, in this case, is the number of years from when the portfolio was created to the time of retirement. This example assumes the investor started to invest at the age of 20 and plans to retire at the age of 65.

- <u>Ending Balance</u> is the calculated value of the portfolio at retirement.

Some examples of Future Value will help to illustrate the relationship of risk and reward.

Table 6. Examples of Future Value

Rate of Return	Initial Investment	Periodic Investment	Number of Periods	Ending Balance
5%	-$10,000	-$1,200	45	$281,490
7%	-$10,000	-$1,200	45	$552,924
10%	-$10,000	-$1,200	45	$1,591,591

The examples in Table 6 show that the higher the rate of return the higher the resulting ending balance. A higher rate of return also indicates a higher level of risk in the portfolio. You must carefully consider the right amount of risk for your situation.

Reward, like Risk, comes in different forms from different investments. Bonds are a loan for which the borrower promises to pay interest to the owner of the bond and agrees to pay back the principal of the bond after a set period of time. Bonds can be called if the issuer of the bond decides to pay off the principal as economic circumstances change. For instance, if interest rates go down, the issuer of the bond can <u>call</u> the bond and then issue new bonds at a lower interest rate. This makes bonds subject to risk that the bond holder, after the bond has been called, may not find an investment with as high a rate of return. With a stock, the investor has an equity stake in the corporation that issued the stock. The stock holder is a part owner of the corporation and has limited input through proxies in the operation of the corporation. If the corporation is successful, the stock holder may receive dividends, and the price of the stock may go up. The stock holder can sell the stock at any time for the current price.

TABLES AND EXPLANATIONS

Tables 7 through 11 are the heart of this book. <u>They show the relationship between risk and reward.</u> **They are <u>not</u> intended to show the value of <u>your</u> portfolio at any given time.** The tables do not consider the following:

- Taxes on dividends or capital gains;
- Investment Costs;
- Selection of Securities;
- The current health of the economy;
- **The results from these tables cannot be taken as an indication of future results.**

The tables use real historical market data from 1928 to 2021. Covering such a long period of time makes the tables useful to decide the asset allocation that may be best for you. This **does not** mean the average gain in future years will be the same as the average gain in the tables.

It is easy to see the relationship of risk and reward when studying Table 7, which shows that Stocks have been more volatile than Bonds, and Bonds have been more volatile than Treasury Bills. Table 7 also shows that Stocks have provided more reward than Bonds, and Bonds have provided more reward than Treasury Bills over the years covered in the table.

Table 7 shows that Stocks had 25 losing years out of 94. There were also four times that Stocks had consecutive year losses. The longest of these was four years, from 1929 to 1932. There was also a three year period of losses, from 2000 to 2002. Along with the consecutive losses, there were several deep, single year losses. Bonds had only two consecutive periods of loss consisting of two years, from 1956 to 1957 and 1979 to 1980, and the single year losses were not as severe. Bonds had 15 losing years out of the 94.

Table 8 shows the results of a portfolio with 60% Stocks and 40% Bonds. This has long been the most popular asset allocation among financial advisors.

Table 9 shows the results of a portfolio with 70% Stocks and 30% Bonds. This allocation is becoming more popular. Table 10 shows the results of a portfolio with 80% Stocks and 20% Bonds. Table 11 shows the results of a portfolio with 80% Stock and 20% Treasury Bills.

Tables 8 through 11 start with an investment of $10,000, and no additional investment. Row one of Tables 8 through 11 shows the beginning stock, bond or cash, and portfolio balances. Stock and bond returns for each year are calculated by multiplying the prior year balance by their respective return rates. The new balances for stocks and bonds are calculated by adding their respective returns to their previous balances. Portfolio balance is the sum of the Stock Balance and the Bond Balance.

The annual return rate data in these Tables 7 thru 11 are as follows:

Stocks - S&P 500 (including dividends)
Bonds - Baa Corporate Bond
TBill - 3-month Treasury Bills

Table 7. Market Returns Show Risk and Reward

	Stocks	Bonds	TBills		Stocks	Bonds	TBills		Stocks	Bonds	TBills
1928	43.81%	3.22%	3.08%	**1957**	-10.46%	-0.72%	3.23%	**1986**	18.49%	21.49%	5.98%
1929	-8.30%	3.02%	3.16%	**1958**	43.72%	6.43%	1.77%	**1987**	5.81%	2.29%	5.78%
1930	-25.12%	0.54%	4.55%	**1959**	12.06%	1.57%	3.39%	**1988**	16.54%	15.12%	6.67%
1931	-43.84%	-15.68%	2.31%	**1960**	0.34%	6.66%	2.88%	**1989**	31.48%	15.79%	8.11%
1932	-8.64%	23.59%	1.07%	**1961**	26.64%	5.10%	2.35%	**1990**	-3.06%	6.14%	7.49%
1933	49.98%	12.97%	0.96%	**1962**	-8.81%	6.50%	2.77%	**1991**	30.23%	17.85%	5.38%
1934	-1.19%	18.82%	0.28%	**1963**	22.61%	5.46%	3.16%	**1992**	7.49%	12.17%	3.43%
1935	46.74%	13.31%	0.17%	**1964**	16.42%	5.16%	3.55%	**1993**	9.97%	16.43%	3.00%
1936	31.94%	11.38%	0.17%	**1965**	12.40%	3.19%	3.95%	**1994**	1.33%	-1.32%	4.25%
1937	-35.34%	-4.42%	0.28%	**1966**	-9.97%	-3.45%	4.86%	**1995**	37.20%	20.16%	5.49%
1938	29.28%	9.24%	0.07%	**1967**	23.80%	0.90%	4.31%	**1996**	22.68%	4.79%	5.01%
1939	-1.10%	7.98%	0.05%	**1968**	10.81%	4.85%	5.34%	**1997**	33.10%	11.83%	5.06%
1940	-10.67%	8.65%	0.04%	**1969**	-8.24%	-2.03%	6.67%	**1998**	28.34%	7.95%	4.78%
1941	-12.77%	5.01%	0.13%	**1970**	3.56%	5.65%	6.39%	**1999**	20.89%	0.84%	4.64%
1942	19.17%	5.18%	0.34%	**1971**	14.22%	14.00%	4.33%	**2000**	-9.03%	9.33%	5.82%
1943	25.06%	8.04%	0.38%	**1972**	18.76%	11.41%	4.07%	**2001**	-11.85%	7.82%	3.39%
1944	19.03%	6.57%	0.38%	**1973**	-14.31%	4.32%	7.03%	**2002**	-21.97%	12.18%	1.60%
1945	35.82%	6.80%	0.38%	**1974**	-25.90%	-4.38%	7.83%	**2003**	28.36%	13.53%	1.01%
1946	-8.43%	2.51%	0.38%	**1975**	37.00%	11.05%	5.78%	**2004**	10.74%	9.89%	1.37%
1947	5.20%	0.26%	0.60%	**1976**	23.83%	19.75%	4.97%	**2005**	4.83%	4.92%	3.15%
1948	5.70%	3.44%	1.05%	**1977**	-6.98%	9.95%	5.27%	**2006**	15.61%	7.05%	4.73%
1949	18.30%	5.38%	1.12%	**1978**	6.51%	3.14%	7.19%	**2007**	5.48%	3.15%	4.35%
1950	30.81%	4.24%	1.20%	**1979**	18.52%	-2.01%	10.07%	**2008**	-36.55%	-5.07%	1.37%
1951	23.68%	-0.19%	1.52%	**1980**	31.74%	-3.32%	11.43%	**2009**	25.94%	23.33%	0.15%
1952	18.15%	4.44%	1.72%	**1981**	-4.70%	8.46%	14.03%	**2010**	14.82%	8.35%	0.14%
1953	-1.21%	1.62%	1.89%	**1982**	20.42%	29.05%	10.61%	**2011**	2.10%	12.58%	0.05%
1954	52.56%	6.16%	0.94%	**1983**	22.34%	16.19%	8.61%	**2012**	15.89%	10.12%	0.09%
1955	32.60%	2.04%	1.73%	**1984**	6.15%	15.62%	9.52%	**2013**	32.15%	-1.06%	0.06%
1956	7.44%	-2.35%	2.63%	**1985**	31.24%	23.86%	7.48%	**2014**	13.52%	10.38%	0.03%

Table 7. Continued

	Stocks	Bonds	TBills		Stocks	Bonds	TBills
2015	1.38%	-0.70%	0.05%	**2019**	31.21%	15.33%	1.55%
2016	11.77%	10.37%	0.32%	**2020**	18.01%	10.41%	0.09%
2017	21.61%	9.72%	0.93%	**2021**	28.47%	0.93%	0.06%
2018	-4.23%	-2.76%	1.94%				

The Market Returns for Stocks, Bonds, and TBills in Tables 7 through 11 are actual U. S. Market Data from *Damodaran Online*. Aswath Damoraran is a Professor of Finance at the Stern School of Business at New York University.

There were four times that stocks had consecutive year losses. In each of these cases there were substantial gains in either the next year or the next two years. This suggests the following conclusions:

- Buy and Hold is a worthwhile strategy
- Holding enough cash to avoid selling during these periods merits consideration

The average return for Stocks from 1928 to 2021 was 11.82%. The average return for Bonds was 7.19% and the average return for TBills was 3.33%.

A Case for Buy and Hold

The stock market returns I have researched for this analysis are the returns from the S&P 500. In analyzing them I have looked at five, ten, fifteen, and twenty year groups from each of the 94 years. I have calculated the average returns of each of these groups.

Year by Year

The S&P 500 had an average return of 11.82% over the 94 years from 1928 to 2021. Out of the 94 years, there were 25 single year losses.

Five Year Groups

The overall average return for each average five-year return for the S&P 500 over 94 years was 11.74%. Six of the five-year groups had losses.

Ten Year Groups

None of the ten-year groups had an average loss. The average return for the ten-year groups was 11.92%.

Fifteen Year Groups

None of the fifteen-year groups had an average loss. The average return for the fifteen-year groups was 12.03%.

Twenty Year Groups

None of the twenty-year groups had an average loss. The average returns for the twenty-year groups was 12.25%.

Conclusion

The preceding market results clearly show that during the period of 1928 to 2021, the longer a portfolio consisting of an "Index" of S&P 500 stocks was held, the less the risk and the greater the return. In fact, there were no losses when these investments were held for ten years or more.

This suggests a "buy and hold" investment policy. However, it is important to acknowledge that past is not prolog. In other words, the results from the past may suggest a safe and rewarding investment policy, but circumstances change. There is no sure thing.

Table 8. Stocks 60% and Bonds 40% over 45 Years

Year	Stock Return %	Stock Return $	Stock Balance	Bond Return %	Bond Return $	Bond Balance	Portfolio Balance
			$6,000			$4,000	$10,000
1977	-6.98%	-$419	$5,581	9.95%	$398	$4,398	$9,979
1978	6.51%	$363	$5,945	3.14%	$138	$4,536	$10,481
1979	18.52%	$1,101	$7,045	-2.01%	-$91	$4,445	$11,490
1980	31.74%	$2,236	$9,282	-3.32%	-$148	$4,297	$13,579
1981	-4.70%	-$436	$8,845	8.46%	$364	$4,661	$13,506
1982	20.42%	$1,806	$10,652	29.05%	$1,354	$6,015	$16,667
1983	22.34%	$2,380	$13,031	16.19%	$974	$6,989	$20,020
1984	6.15%	$801	$13,833	15.62%	$1,092	$8,080	$21,913
1985	31.24%	$4,321	$18,154	23.86%	$1,928	$10,008	$28,162
1986	18.49%	$3,357	$21,511	21.49%	$2,151	$12,159	$33,670
1987	5.81%	$1,250	$22,761	2.29%	$278	$12,438	$35,198
1988	16.54%	$3,765	$26,525	15.12%	$1,881	$14,318	$40,843
1989	31.48%	$8,350	$34,875	15.79%	$2,261	$16,579	$51,454
1990	-3.06%	-$1,067	$33,808	6.14%	$1,018	$17,597	$51,405
1991	30.23%	$10,220	$44,028	17.85%	$3,141	$20,738	$64,766
1992	7.49%	$3,298	$47,326	12.17%	$2,524	$23,262	$70,588
1993	9.97%	$4,718	$52,044	16.43%	$3,822	$27,084	$79,128
1994	1.33%	$692	$52,736	-1.32%	-$358	$26,726	$79,463
1995	37.20%	$19,618	$72,354	20.16%	$5,388	$32,114	$104,469
1996	22.68%	$16,410	$88,764	4.79%	$1,538	$33,652	$122,417
1997	33.10%	$29,381	$118,145	11.83%	$3,981	$37,633	$155,779
1998	28.34%	$33,482	$151,628	7.95%	$2,992	$40,625	$192,253
1999	20.89%	$31,675	$183,303	0.84%	$341	$40,967	$224,269
2000	-9.03%	-$16,552	$166,751	9.33%	$3,822	$44,789	$211,539

Table 8. Continued

Year	Stock Return Rate	Stock Return $	Stock Balance	Bond Return Rate	Bond Return $	Bond Balance	Portfolio Balance
2001	-11.85%	-$24,469	$182,019	7.82%	$4,194	$57,829	$239,847
2002	-21.97%	-$39,989	$142,029	12.18%	$7,044	$64,872	$206,901
2003	28.36%	$40,279	$182,309	13.53%	$8,777	$73,650	$255,958
2004	10.74%	$19,580	$201,888	9.89%	$7,284	$80,933	$282,822
2005	4.83%	$9,751	$211,640	4.92%	$3,982	$84,915	$296,555
2006	15.61%	$33,037	$244,677	7.05%	$5,987	$90,902	$335,579
2007	5.46%	$13,359	$258,036	3.15%	$2,863	$93,765	$351,801
2008	-36.55%	-$94,312	$163,724	-5.07%	-$4,754	$89,011	$252,735
2009	25.94%	$42,470	$206,194	23.33%	$20,766	$109,778	$315,972
2010	14.82%	$30,558	$236,752	8.35%	$9,166	$118,944	$355,696
2011	2.10%	$4,972	$241,724	12.58%	$14,963	$133,907	$375,631
2012	15.89%	$38,410	$280,133	10.12%	$13,551	$147,459	$427,592
2013	32.15%	$90,063	$370,196	-1.06%	-$1,563	$145,896	$516,092
2014	13.52%	$50,051	$420,247	10.38%	$15,144	$161,040	$581,287
2015	1.38%	$5,799	$426,046	-0.70%	-$1,127	$159,913	$585,959
2016	11.77%	$50,146	$476,192	10.37%	$16,583	$176,495	$652,687
2017	21.61%	$102,905	$579,097	9.72%	$17,155	$193,651	$772,748
2018	-4.23%	-$24,496	$554,601	-2.76%	-$5,345	$188,306	$742,907
2019	31.21%	$173,091	$727,692	15.33%	$28,867	$217,173	$944,865
2020	18.01%	$131,057	$858,749	10.41%	$22,608	$239,781	$1,098,531
2021	28.47%	$244,486	$1,103,235	0.93%	$2,230	$242,011	$1,345,247

With an investment of $10,000, the 60/40 allocation, stocks gained $1,097,235 in the 45 years between 1977 and 2021. Bonds gained $238,011 in the same time period. In total, the portfolio went from $10,000 to $1,345,247, a gain of $1,335,247 over 45 years.

Table 9. Stocks 70% and Bonds 30% over 45 years

Year	Stock Return Pct	Stock Return $	Stock Balance	Bond Return Pct	Bond Return $	Bond Balance	Portfolio Balance
			$7,000			$3,000	$10,000
1977	-6.98%	-$489	$6,511	9.95%	$299	$3,299	$9,810
1978	6.51%	$424	$6,935	3.14%	$104	$3,402	$10,337
1979	18.52%	$1,284	$8,220	-2.01%	-$68	$3,334	$11,553
1980	31.74%	$2,609	$10,829	-3.32%	-$111	$3,223	$14,052
1981	-4.70%	-$509	$10,320	8.46%	$273	$3,496	$13,815
1982	20.42%	$2,107	$12,427	29.05%	$1,015	$4,511	$16,938
1983	22.34%	$2,776	$15,203	16.19%	$730	$5,242	$20,445
1984	6.15%	$935	$16,138	15.62%	$819	$6,060	$22,198
1985	31.24%	$5,042	$21,180	23.86%	$1,446	$7,506	$28,686
1986	18.49%	$3,916	$25,096	21.49%	$1,613	$9,119	$34,215
1987	5.81%	$1,458	$26,554	2.29%	$209	$9,328	$35,882
1988	16.54%	$4,392	$30,946	15.12%	$1,410	$10,739	$41,685
1989	31.48%	$9,742	$40,688	15.79%	$1,696	$12,434	$53,122
1990	-3.06%	-$1,245	$39,443	6.14%	$763	$13,198	$52,640
1991	30.23%	$11,924	$51,366	17.85%	$2,356	$15,553	$66,920
1992	7.49%	$3,847	$55,214	12.17%	$1,893	$17,446	$72,660
1993	9.97%	$5,505	$60,718	16.43%	$2,866	$20,313	$81,031
1994	1.33%	$808	$61,526	-1.32%	-$268	$20,045	$81,570
1995	37.20%	$22,888	$84,413	20.16%	$4,041	$24,086	$108,499
1996	22.68%	$19,145	$103,558	4.79%	$1,154	$25,239	$128,798
1997	33.10%	$34,278	$137,836	11.83%	$2,986	$28,225	$166,061
1998	28.34%	$39,063	$176,899	7.95%	$2,244	$30,469	$207,368
1999	20.89%	$36,954	$213,853	0.84%	$256	$30,725	$244,578
2000	-9.03%	-$19,311	$194,542	9.33%	$2,867	$33,592	$228,134

Table 9. Continued

Year	Stock Return Rate	Stock Return $	Stock Balance	Bond Return Rate	Bond Return $	Bond Balance	Portfolio Balance
2001	-11.85%	-$28,547	$212,355	7.82%	$3,146	$43,372	$255,727
2002	-21.97%	-$46,654	$165,701	12.18%	$5,283	$48,654	$214,355
2003	28.36%	$46,993	$212,693	13.53%	$6,583	$55,237	$267,930
2004	10.74%	$22,843	$235,537	9.89%	$5,463	$60,700	$296,237
2005	4.83%	$11,376	$246,913	4.92%	$2,986	$63,687	$310,600
2006	15.61%	$38,543	$285,456	7.05%	$4,490	$68,176	$353,633
2007	5.48%	$15,643	$301,099	3.15%	$2,148	$70,324	$371,423
2008	-36.55%	-$110,052	$191,047	-5.07%	-$3,565	$66,759	$257,806
2009	25.94%	$49,558	$240,605	23.33%	$15,575	$82,333	$322,938
2010	14.82%	$35,658	$276,263	8.35%	$6,875	$89,208	$365,471
2011	2.10%	$5,802	$282,064	12.58%	$11,222	$100,431	$382,495
2012	15.89%	$44,820	$326,884	10.12%	$10,164	$110,594	$437,478
2013	32.15%	$105,093	$431,978	-1.06%	-$1,172	$109,422	$541,399
2014	13.52%	$58,403	$490,381	10.38%	$11,358	$120,780	$611,161
2015	1.38%	$6,767	$497,148	-0.70%	-$845	$119,934	$617,083
2016	11.77%	$58,514	$555,663	10.37%	$12,437	$132,372	$688,034
2017	21.61%	$120,079	$675,741	9.72%	$12,867	$145,238	$820,979
2018	-4.23%	-$28,584	$647,157	-2.76%	-$4,009	$141,230	$788,387
2019	31.21%	$201,978	$849,135	15.33%	$21,650	$162,880	$1,012,015
2020	18.01%	$152,929	$1,002,064	10.41%	$16,956	$179,836	$1,181,900
2021	28.47%	$285,288	$1,287,352	0.93%	$1,672	$181,508	$1,468,860

In 45 years stocks gained $1,280,352 with the 70/30 Allocation while bonds gained $178,508. The total gain was $1,458,860, which was $123,613 more than with the 60/40 Allocation.

Table 10. Stocks 80% and Bonds 20% over 45 years

Year	Stock Return %	Stock Return $	Stock Balance	Bond Return %	Bond Return $	Bond Balance	Portfolio Balance
			$8,000			$2,000	$10,000
1977	-6.98%	-$558	$7,442	9.95%	$199	$2,199	$9,641
1978	6.51%	$484	$7,926	3.14%	$69	$2,268	$10,194
1979	18.52%	$1,468	$9,394	-2.01%	-$46	$2,222	$11,616
1980	31.74%	$2,982	$12,376	-3.32%	-$74	$2,149	$14,524
1981	-4.70%	-$582	$11,794	8.46%	$182	$2,330	$14,124
1982	20.42%	$2,408	$14,202	29.05%	$677	$3,007	$17,210
1983	22.34%	$3,173	$17,375	16.19%	$487	$3,494	$20,869
1984	6.15%	$1,069	$18,444	15.62%	$546	$4,040	$22,484
1985	31.24%	$5,762	$24,205	23.86%	$964	$5,004	$29,210
1986	18.49%	$4,476	$28,681	21.49%	$1,075	$6,080	$34,761
1987	5.81%	$1,666	$30,347	2.29%	$139	$6,219	$36,566
1988	16.54%	$5,019	$35,367	15.12%	$940	$7,159	$42,526
1989	31.48%	$11,133	$46,500	15.79%	$1,130	$8,289	$54,790
1990	-3.06%	-$1,423	$45,077	6.14%	$509	$8,798	$53,876
1991	30.23%	$13,627	$58,704	17.85%	$1,571	$10,369	$69,073
1992	7.49%	$4,397	$63,101	12.17%	$1,262	$11,631	$74,732
1993	9.97%	$6,291	$69,392	16.43%	$1,911	$13,542	$82,934
1994	1.33%	$923	$70,315	-1.32%	-$179	$13,363	$83,678
1995	37.20%	$26,157	$96,473	20.16%	$2,694	$16,057	$112,530
1996	22.68%	$21,880	$118,353	4.79%	$769	$16,826	$135,179
1997	33.10%	$39,175	$157,527	11.83%	$1,991	$18,817	$176,344
1998	28.34%	$44,643	$202,170	7.95%	$1,496	$20,313	$222,483
1999	20.89%	$42,233	$244,404	0.84%	$171	$20,483	$264,887
2000	-9.03%	-$22,070	$222,334	9.33%	$1,911	$22,394	$244,729

Table 10. Continued

Year	Stock Return Rate	Stock Return $	Stock Balance	Bond Return Rate	Bond Return $	Bond Balance	Portfolio Balance
2001	-11.85%	-$32,625	$242,691	7.82%	$2,097	$28,914	$271,606
2002	-21.97%	-$53,319	$189,372	12.18%	$3,522	$32,436	$221,808
2003	28.36%	$53,706	$243,078	13.53%	$4,389	$36,825	$279,903
2004	10.74%	$26,107	$269,185	9.89%	$3,642	$40,467	$309,651
2005	4.83%	$13,002	$282,186	4.92%	$1,991	$42,458	$324,644
2006	15.61%	$44,049	$326,236	7.05%	$2,993	$45,451	$371,687
2007	5.48%	$17,878	$344,113	3.15%	$1,432	$46,883	$390,996
2008	-36.55%	-$125,773	$218,340	-5.07%	-$2,377	$44,506	$262,846
2009	25.94%	$56,637	$274,977	23.33%	$10,383	$54,889	$329,866
2010	14.82%	$40,752	$315,729	8.35%	$4,583	$59,472	$375,201
2011	2.10%	$6,630	$322,359	12.58%	$7,482	$66,954	$389,313
2012	15.89%	$51,223	$373,582	10.12%	$6,776	$73,729	$447,311
2013	32.15%	$120,107	$493,689	-1.06%	-$782	$72,948	$566,637
2014	13.52%	$66,747	$560,435	10.38%	$7,572	$80,520	$640,955
2015	1.38%	$7,734	$568,169	-0.70%	-$564	$79,956	$648,126
2016	11.77%	$66,874	$635,043	10.37%	$8,291	$88,248	$723,291
2017	21.61%	$137,233	$772,276	9.72%	$8,578	$96,825	$869,101
2018	-4.23%	-$32,667	$739,608	-2.76%	-$2,672	$94,153	$833,761
2019	31.21%	$230,832	$970,440	15.33%	$14,434	$108,587	$1,079,027
2020	18.01%	$174,776	$1,145,216	10.41%	$11,304	$119,891	$1,265,107
2021	28.47%	$326,043	$1,471,260	0.93%	$1,115	$121,006	$1,592,265

With an 80/20 allocation, stocks gained $1,463,260 and bonds gained $119,006 for a total portfolio gain of $1,582,266.

Table 11. Stocks 80% and TBills 20% over 45 years

Year	Total Return TBills %	TBill Return $	Investment $	TBill Balance	Stock Return %	Stock Return $	Stock Balance	Total Balance
				$2,000			$8,000	$10,000
1977	5.27%	$105	$0	$2,105	-6.98%	-$558	$7,442	$9,547
1978	7.19%	$151	$0	$2,257	6.51%	$484	$7,926	$10,183
1979	10.07%	$227	$0	$2,484	18.52%	$1,468	$9,394	$27,022
1980	11.43%	$284	$0	$2,768	31.74%	$2,982	$12,376	$15,144
1981	14.03%	$388	$0	$3,156	-4.70%	-$582	$11,794	$14,950
1982	10.61%	$335	$0	$3,491	20.42%	$2,408	$14,202	$17,693
1983	8.61%	$301	$0	$3,792	22.34%	$3,173	$17,375	$21,167
1984	9.52%	$361	$0	$4,153	6.15%	$1,069	$18,444	$22,596
1985	7.48%	$311	$0	$4,463	31.24%	$5,762	$24,205	$28,669
1986	5.98%	$267	$0	$4,730	18.49%	$4,476	$28,681	$33,411
1987	5.78%	$273	$0	$5,004	5.81%	$1,666	$30,347	$35,351
1988	6.67%	$334	$0	$5,337	16.54%	$5,019	$35,367	$40,704
1989	8.11%	$433	$0	$5,770	31.48%	$11,133	$46,500	$52,271
1990	7.49%	$432	$0	$6,203	-3.06%	-$1,423	$45,077	$51,280
1991	5.36%	$332	$0	$6,535	30.23%	$13,627	$58,704	$65,239
1992	3.43%	$224	$0	$6,759	7.49%	$4,397	$63,101	$69,860
1993	3.00%	$203	$0	$6,962	9.97%	$6,291	$69,392	$76,354
1994	4.25%	$296	$0	$7,258	1.33%	$923	$70,315	$77,573
1995	5.49%	$398	$0	$7,656	37.20%	$26,157	$96,473	$104,129
1996	5.01%	$384	$0	$8,040	22.68%	$21,880	$118,353	$126,392
1997	5.06%	$407	$0	$8,447	33.10%	$39,175	$157,527	$165,974
1998	4.78%	$404	$0	$8,850	28.34%	$44,643	$202,170	$211,021
1999	4.64%	$411	$0	$9,261	20.89%	$42,233	$244,404	$253,665
2000	5.82%	$539	$0	$9,800	-9.03%	-$22,070	$222,334	$232,134

Table 11. Continued

Year	TBill Return Rate	TBill Return $	Investment	TBill Balance	Stock Return Rate	Stock Return $	Stock Balance	Portfolio Balance
2001	3.39%	$349	$0	$10,636	-11.85%	-$32,625	$242,691	$253,327
2002	1.60%	$170	$0	$10,806	-21.97%	-$53,319	$189,372	$200,178
2003	1.01%	$109	$0	$10,915	28.36%	$53,706	$243,078	$253,993
2004	1.37%	$150	$0	$11,065	10.74%	$26,107	$269,185	$280,249
2005	3.15%	$349	$0	$11,413	4.83%	$13,002	$282,186	$293,599
2006	4.73%	$540	$0	$11,953	15.61%	$44,049	$326,236	$338,189
2007	4.35%	$520	$0	$12,473	5.48%	$17,878	$344,113	$356,586
2008	1.37%	$171	$0	$12,644	-36.55%	-$125,773	$218,340	$230,984
2009	0.15%	$19	$0	$12,663	25.94%	$56,637	$274,977	$287,640
2010	0.14%	$18	$0	$12,681	14.82%	$40,752	$315,729	$328,409
2011	0.05%	$6	$0	$12,687	2.10%	$6,630	$322,359	$335,046
2012	0.09%	$11	$0	$12,698	15.89%	$51,223	$373,582	$386,280
2013	0.06%	$8	$0	$12,706	32.15%	$120,107	$493,689	$506,395
2014	0.03%	$4	$0	$12,710	13.52%	$66,747	$560,435	$573,145
2015	0.05%	$6	$0	$12,716	1.38%	$7,734	$568,169	$580,885
2016	0.32%	$41	$0	$12,757	11.77%	$66,874	$635,043	$647,800
2017	0.93%	$119	$0	$12,875	21.61%	$137,233	$772,276	$785,151
2018	1.94%	$250	$0	$13,125	-4.23%	-$32,667	$739,608	$752,734
2019	1.55%	$203	$0	$13,329	31.21%	$230,832	$970,440	$983,769
2020	0.09%	$12	$0	$13,341	18.01%	$174,776	$1,145,216	$1,158,557
2021	3.33%	$444	$0	$13,785	28.47%	$326,043	$1,471,260	$1,485,045

With the 80% Stocks 20% TBills allocation, the portfolio gained $1,475,045.

In summary the allocations performed as follows:

- 60% Stock/40% Bonds portfolio grew to $1,345,247;
- 70% Stock/30% Bonds portfolio grew to $1,468,860;
- 80% Stock/20% Bonds portfolio grew to $1,592,266;
- 80% Stock/20% TBill portfolio grew to $1,485,045.

Things to learn from these tables:

- Stocks provide growth, and growth is important over the long term.
- A Buy and Hold strategy (investors maintain a reasonably stable portfolio over a long period of time) is a way to stay invested when the market is doing well or coming back from a downturn. Look at Table 7 to see how the market recovers after consecutive or deep loses. You also save on transaction costs and taxes.

With the information from Table 7 and the knowledge of your typical expenses, you should be able to decide how much of a cash cushion you need to keep on hand.

The investor can use a version of the *Time Value of Money* concept to analyze the results of these tables. Look at the 60% Stocks and 40% Bonds asset allocation in Table 8, which starts with $10,000 and after 45 years ends with $1,345,247.

Columns:
• Present Value = initial investment
• Number of periods = 45
• Future Value = value of the investment after growth
• Payment = $0 needs to be entered if there is no payment
• Rate of Return = automatically calculated

This example is from *Apple Pages* using the Rate function, but other spreadsheets will be similar.

Table 12 Average Yearly Return for Stocks from 1977 to 2021

Present Value	Number of Periods	Future Value	Payments	Rate of Return
-$6,000	45	$1,103,235	$0	12.29%

Table 13. Average Yearly Return for Bonds from 1977 to 2021

Present Value	Number of Periods	Future Value	Payments	Rate of Return
-$4,000	45	$242,011	$0	9.55%

ASSET ALLOCATION EXAMPLES AND REBALANCING

Tables 14 through 17 show the results that different asset allocations would have produced using actual market data during the forty-five years from 1977 to 2021.

Table 14. Average Yearly Return for 60% Stock 40% Bond

Present Value	Number of Periods	Future Value	Payments	Rate of Return
-$10,000	45	$1,345,247	$0	11.51%

Table 15. Average Yearly Return for 70% Stock 30% Bond

Present Value	Number of Periods	Future Value	Payments	Rate of Return
-$10,000	45	$1,468,860	$0	11.73%

Table 16. Average Yearly Return for 80% Stock 20% Bond

Present Value	Number of Periods	Future Value	Payments	Rate of Return
-$10,000	45	$1,592,265	$0	11.93%

Table 17. Average Yearly Return for 80% Stock 20% TBills

Present Value	Number of Periods	Future Value	Payments	Rate of Return
-$10,000	45	$1,485,045	$0	11.75%

Note: When looking at the differences in the average returns, don't forget to look at the differences in Future Values also. Notice it does not take a large increase in the rate of return to make a large difference in the Future Value. Be aware that these returns do not take investment expenses, taxes, or inflation into account. Remember also, the market changes for many reasons and the old saying, "Past is not prologue" is especially true. In other words, don't depend on history repeating itself.

The allocations shown in Tables 14 through 17 are the allocations at the time of investment. Allocations change as the assets have gains and losses. For instance, after 45 years, the 60% Stock and 40% Bond allocation became 82% Stock and 18% Bond. This is logical since stocks had higher returns than bonds during those years. Changes occur with the other allocations also. Historically these changes have increased the risk level over the years. For this reason many financial advisors recommend rebalancing a portfolio periodically.

Rebalancing a Portfolio

Rebalancing a portfolio brings it back to the target allocation. To accomplish this rebalancing, securities in allocations that are overweight are sold, and securities in underweight allocations are purchased. The target allocation may also change over time. The decision to rebalance is personal. Not all investors choose to rebalance their portfolio, and tax consequences should be considered if securities are sold.

Rebalancing can also be achieved without selling assets. By changing the investment strategy, more money can be allocated to underweight securities over time to reach the target allocation.

WHAT ABOUT CASH?

Financial experts have said for many years we should have from three to six months worth of expenses in cash. This belief is changing and many experts are beginning to say we need more cash than that. What are the reasons you need cash in the portfolio?

- Having cash available precludes the necessity to sell securities at an inopportune time, e.g., when stock prices have dropped.

- Having cash keeps you from being forced to sell companies that you do not want to sell and face stiff tax consequences.

- Having cash allows you to take advantage of buying opportunities.

- Having cash helps you get through emergencies without selling assets you want to keep.

- Cash helps to minimize the risk associated with a large position of stock in your portfolio.

Asset Allocation is only part of the reduction of risk. Another part is diversification within your portfolio. You must own investments in different sectors and different companies within those sectors. Another way to obtain this diversification is with index funds which allow you to own the whole market with low expenses. Because of low turnover, they are also tax efficient. Another option is Mutual Funds which are selected stocks from the whole market or from sectors of the market.

Things to keep in mind

• Past investment performance is not a guarantee of future performance.

• Tables showing asset allocations are not a recommendation of which asset allocation to adopt. They are just examples of how these allocations have performed over the past 45 years.

• Investment costs, fees, taxes, and inflation are not considered in the tables.

In general, this book is not a "How-To" for investing. It is intended to give the reader some new perspectives. The reader should study the tables and consider other information to make up his or her mind about the asset allocation and investment policies to adopt.

It is crucial that a young person or couple start saving and investing as early as possible. Examples of *Time Value of Money* indicate how important time is in the accumulation of wealth. A late start to saving and investing is a handicap, but it is never too late to start.

TIMING IS IMPORTANT IN INVESTING

The age you begin to invest makes more of a difference than most people believe. It is logical that the longer you invest money, the more you will accumulate, but the dynamics of compounding in *Time Value of Money* are noteworthy. Here are some examples:

Table 18. Yearly Investments

Years	Average Yearly Rate of Return	Yearly Investment	Ending Balance
15	8%	-$6,000	$162,913
25	8%	-$6,000	$438,636
35	8%	-$6,000	$1,033,901
45	8%	-$6,000	$2,319,034

Table 18 above shows how much an investment of $6,000 each year will grow to in 15, 25, 35, and 45 years.

Table 19. Monthly Investments

Months of Investment	Average Monthly Rate of Return	Investment per Month	Ending Balance
180	0.67%	-$500	$173,634
300	0.67%	-$500	$478,616
420	0.67%	-$500	$1,158,262
540	0.67%	-$500	$2,672,839

Table 19 shows the result of investing $500 each month. The results of investing every month compared to the results of investing once a year over an extended period makes quite a difference.

After adjusting the table from yearly investments to monthly investments, the yearly amount of $6,000 remains the same. The yearly rate of return also remains at 8%.

Tables 18 and 19 show the earlier you start to invest and the more regularly you invest, the better chance you will have to reach your goals. These tables are for illustrative purposes only.

Investment Policy

A savvy investor creates and periodically updates an investment policy, a set of guidelines that you think are appropriate for your situation. The policy does not need to be long or complicated, and it should be constructed and reviewed with your investment advisor, if you are working with one.

Investment Policy Example

- Objectives - The portfolio should focus on growth and preserving the long-term real purchasing power of the assets.

- Asset Allocation (see page 25)

Equity	65 to 85%
*U.S. 90 to 95%	
*Foreign 5 to 10%	
Fixed Income	5 to 10%
Cash and Equivalents	10 to 30%

*Percentage of Equity

Other investment policy issues:

- Aim for a rate of 6% return (after investment costs, taxes and inflation);

- Review the policy each year, and update when necessary;

- Keep the selling of securities to a minimum with attention to investment costs and tax consequences;

- No purchase of securities on margin or executing short sales;

- No purchase of derivative securities for speculation or leverage;

- No individual company should represent more than 10% of the value of the portfolio;

This Investment policy is just an example. Your investment policy should reflect <u>your</u> goals and <u>your</u> views about risk and reward.

SUMMARY

Start to save and invest as early as possible

Risk

Table 7 shows that Stocks have more risk than Bonds, and Bonds have more risk than Treasury Bills (cash equivalents).

Researching the Beta of a security is a good way to determine the risk of an individual investment.

Asset allocation and diversification of your investments are important to mitigate risk in your portfolio.

Reward

Table 7 also shows that stocks provide a higher return than bonds, and bonds provide a higher return than treasury bills. Although stocks offer a greater return, they also have greater volatility than bonds and cash.

Asset Allocation

Table 8 shows the results of a 60% Stock 40% Bond allocation, Table 9 shows a 70% Stock 30% Bond allocation, Table 10 shows an 80% Stock 20% Bond allocation, Table 11 shows an allocation of 80% Stock and 20% TBills. The Tables demonstrate the risk and reward with each different allocation.

Thoroughly research the securities you intend to invest in or to sell. Transaction costs and taxes add up and reduce your return. Buy and sell securities only for a good reason. Do not invest in anything you do not understand.

Taxes

When you sell a security, if you have a gain, you will most likely pay capital gains tax. You also pay tax on any dividends you receive. For complete tax information, including information about early withdrawals and Required Minimum Distributions (RMDs) from retirement accounts, consult a tax accountant.

Cash or Cash Equivalents

Cash in your portfolio reduces risk. It allows you to buy when the market is down, and it also reduces the need to sell when the market is down, or in an emergency situation.

Record Keeping

Get one of the inexpensive budget software programs like *Quicken* or a free software program like *Personal Capital*.

Monitor your Plan

Good record keeping with one of the programs, like the ones mentioned above, can save you from a bad situation such as overspending or underspending during your retirement.

RESEARCHING A COMPANY

Although it is not possible for most of us to visit the companies we invest in and to ask questions of the officers of the company, you need to know as much about the company as possible. It would be helpful if you have used some of the products and services sold by the company. There are many websites that provide research about companies such as:

- Your own brokerage company website
- sec.gov (Edgar)
- Zachs
- Maketwatch

Edgar is a part of the Securities Exchange Commission of the Federal Government. When you access their website (sec.gov), click "Company Filings" under the *Search* prompt. There you will find instructions how to get information about the company you are interested in. Edgar can be overwhelming at first, but it contains a great deal of information about all publicly traded stocks and mutual funds, and the site is well worth the time to explore.

The most complete information about stocks can be found in companies 10-K. The 10-K contains information about a company's revenues, management, future plans, risks, financial data, competition and current operations. The staff at Edgar have done a good job at making information accessible and understandable. You will also find good information about investing in general under the "Education" tab in Edgar.

Researching a company is just that. Company data are not always the complete reason a company's stock price goes up or down. Investor sentiment about the economy, market, and the company itself are part of the picture. Do the best research possible, but be aware that other factors are involved. Beware of Meme stocks because hype on social media can make them volatile and overvalued.

Before starting fundamental analysis you should have a good picture of the U. S. and Global economy. Websites to review are:

- The Bureau of Economic Analysis (<u>bea.gov</u>) which has a number of reports such as: Gross Domestic Product, Personal Income and Outlays, U. S. International Transactions, U. S. International Investment Position; and

- The Bureau of Labor Statistics (<u>bls.gov</u>) website also has a number of reports such as employment reports and the Consumer Price Index.

Financial Statements

The U. S. Securities and Exchange Commission (SEC) gives an excellent overview of financial statements in the Investor Information section of their website, <u>sec.gov</u>.

In their discussion of financial statements they say: "There are four main financial statements. They are: (1) balance sheets; (2) income statements; (3) cash flow statements; and (4) statements of shareholders equity. Balance sheets show what a company owns and what it owes at a fixed point in time. Income statements show how much money a company made and spent over a period of time. Cash flow statements show the exchange of money between a company and the outside world also over a period of time. The fourth financial statement, called a 'statement of shareholders' equity, shows changes in the interests of the company's shareholders over time."

These financial statements are the first source for data used in the research and analysis of companies. Be aware that reading the **footnotes** to the financial statements is extremely important because they often reveal potential problems. The financial statements should be used for trend analysis and ratio analysis.

Trend Analysis

Looking at specific items on a financial statement, such as "Revenue" over a number of years to determine if revenue is increasing or decreasing, is an example of trend analysis. Pay attention to the following items on the statements:

- Sales/Revenue ✓
- Cost of Goods Sold ✓
- Research and Development ✓
- Net Income ✓
- Earnings Per Share (EPS)
- Cash and Short Term Investments
- Accounts Receivable
- Current Assets ✓
- Inventories
- Total Assets
- Long-Term Debt ✓
- Current Liabilities ✓
- Retained Earnings
- Total Equity
- Liabilities and Shareholders Equity
- Net Operating Cash Flow
- Free Cash Flow ✓

This is a long list. If you are short on time, the items with a check mark are the ones I would consider first.

Ratio Analysis

A single ratio is not useful. To be useful, the ratio must be compared with ratios of other companies in similar industries and/or with an Index such as the S&P 500. It is also useful to look at ratio trends for the same company. The following is a set of ratios useful to evaluate stocks. Included are formulas for each ratio and how the results are evaluated. The ratios are divided into four sections: (1) Valuation Ratios; (2) Financial Health Ratios; (3) Profitability Ratios; and (4) Management Efficiency Ratios. The source of the data for calculating the ratios is the financial statements for the company. Ratios already calculated can be found on some financial websites.

<u>Valuation Ratios</u>

- Price/Earnings Ratio (P/E ratio) = Stock Price per Share divided by Earnings per Share. *The ratio should be low.*

- Price/Cash Flow Ratio = Stock Price per Share divided by Operating Cash Flow per Share. This ratio compares the stock's price to the amount of cash flow generated per share. *The lower the number the better.*

- Price/Sales Ratio = Stock Price per Share divided by Net Sales per Share. This ratio gives the amount paid for every dollar of sales. *The lower the better.*

Financial Health Ratios

- Debt/Equity Ratio = Total Liabilities divided by Shareholder's Equity. This datum compares the company's total liabilities to shareholders' equity. *The lower the percentage, the stronger the equity position, but the less leverage used by the company.*

- Current Ratio = Current Assets divided by Current Liabilities. This datum shows the availability of current assets to pay off current liabilities. *The higher the number, the better able the company to pay off current liabilities.*

Profitability Ratios

- Gross Profit Margin = (Net Sales minus Cost of Goods Sold) divided by Net Sales. This ratio gives the amount of profit as a percentage of sales. *The higher the number the better.*

- Return on Equity = Net Income divided by Average Shareholders' Equity. *The higher the ratio, the more efficiently management uses resources provided by shareholders.*

- Return on Assets = Net Income divided by Average Total Assets. *The higher the ratio, the more efficiently management uses the company's assets.*

- Return on Capital = Net Income divided by Capital. *The higher the ratio, the better management generates revenue from its available capital.*

<u>Management Efficiency Ratios</u>

- Receivable Turnover = Net Credit Sales divided by Average Accounts Receivable. *A low ratio implies the company must address its credit policies to ensure timely collection of its receivables.*

- Inventory Turnover = Cost of Goods Sold divided by Average Inventory. *A low turnover may imply weak sales. A high turnover usually implies strong sales or, possibly, inefficient buying practices.*

The following are examples of Ratio and Trend Analysis. The company is fictitious, but the data are realistic.

Table 20. Key Statistics for Company x

	Company X	Industry	S&P 500
Current P/E Ratio	10.8	11.4	18.3
Price/Cash Flow Ratio	7.20	7.50	12.60
Price/Sales Ratio	0.85	1.40	2.14
Gross Profit Margin %	26.9	27.9	34.7
Debt/Equity Ratio	0.09	0.22	2.10
Current Ratio	1.2	1.4	1.2
Return on Equity %	25.4	24.0	25.0
Return on Assets %	13.3	12.1	8.3
Return on Capital %	17.1	16.5	11.1
Receivable Turnover	11.2	14.6	13.7
Inventory Turnover	32.9	14.8	10.2

Table 21. Financial Statement Trends
(in millions except DEPS) data)

	2020	2019	2018	2017	2016
Net Income $	18,688	17,138	14,099	13,328	7,230
Diluted EPS $	8.77	7.80	6.54	6.28	3.48
Long-Term Debt $	5,664	7,405	-	-	-
Cash Flow $	7,362	10,493	10,043	9,291	4,266

The Valuation Ratios compare favorably to the Industry and to the S&P 500 except for Gross Profit Margin. All of Company X's Profitability Ratios are better than both the Industry and the S&P 500. Net Income and Diluted Earnings per Share (DEPS) both trended steadily upward. The ratios indicate good financial strength. Long-term Debt decreased in 2020. Cash Flow was lower in 2020 after trending upward from 2016.

Qualitative Analysis for Company X

In its 10-K, Company X says the company continues to experience an increase in certain costs that exceed the general trend of inflation. The company's operational costs may also be affected by changing economic, regulatory, and political environments in the countries where it operates. Earnings are closely aligned with price levels for the industry. The company's margins may be influenced by inventory levels and geopolitical events.

Final thoughts about Company X

The ratios for company X are generally good. The Financial Statement Trends are also good with the exception of Cash Flow in 2020. More research is needed to determine if this is an ongoing problem. The sentence about the company's operational costs and the sentence about the company's margins in the company's 10-K are concerning. Warnings from a company in its 10-K report should be taken seriously.

Analyzing Bonds

The above analysis was intended for the possible purchase of stocks of the company. Analysis of the company for the purchase of corporate bonds is almost the same. A successful company will make consistent profit which you will share if you hold its stock, or enable them to pay you interest and repay your loan if you hold its bonds.

Additional issues with purchasing bonds

Price - bonds can sell at a discount, a price lower than its face value. This usually indicates the bond is paying a lower interest rate than the prevailing interest rate for similar bonds, and the company is forced to sell the bonds at the lower price. Selling at a premium is just the opposite.

Interest Rate - companies pay interest at periodic intervals. Interest rates can be fixed, floating, payable at maturity, or zero, in the case of zero-coupon bonds. Zero-coupon bonds are sold at a substantial discount to compensate for the lack of interest payments.

<u>Yield</u> - the annual return on the total amount paid for a bond is called the current yield. The total amount you receive holding the bond to maturity is called yield-to-maturity. This calculation allows you to compare different bonds with varying maturities and interest rates.

- Current yield = Interest Rate / Purchase Price

- Yield to Maturity = Total return at maturity including all interest, coupon payments, and premium or discount adjustments. Yield to Maturity calculators can be found on the internet.

<u>Maturity</u> - the date your principal will be repaid. Maturity is an important factor in the risk associated with the bond. Bonds with longer maturities have more risk to changes in interest rates. If the interest rates rise before the maturity of your bond, you lose the opportunity to purchase another bond with the current higher interest rate. If the interest rates fall, you run the risk of the bond you hold being "called" in order for the insurer of the bond to redeem your bond and issue it again at a lower interest rate.

Types of Bonds

- **Corporate Bonds** which are issued by both private and public companies are subject to federal and state taxes.

- **Government Bonds** are issued by the federal government and are subject to federal tax, but exempt from state and local tax.

- **Agency Bonds** are government sponsored and provide funding for federal mortgage, education, agricultural, and other programs. They are exempt from state and local taxes, but subject to federal tax.

- **Municipal Bonds** are issued to fund local projects by states, cities and counties. They are free from federal tax and sometimes also free from state tax.

MUTUAL FUNDS, INDEX FUNDS, AND ETFS

Actively Managed Mutual Funds

An actively managed mutual fund employs portfolio managers who select stocks they think will perform well. The group of stocks that are selected are then professionally managed by the fund. The management of the fund buys and sells stocks in the fund as they see fit, and the fund charges a fee for the management service. The stocks can be from the market as a whole or from a particular sector of the market. Be aware of management costs and fees; they tend to be much higher than index funds. Be sure when you pay these premiums, you get an increase in return that is commensurate with the higher costs.

Index Funds

An Index Fund is sometimes called a "Passive Index Fund" because an index fund buys all the shares of a particular index, or it buys shares of the complete market. Because an Index Fund does not need to have a manager or a team of managers to actively select individual stocks, the expenses for an Index Fund are less. An Index Fund also employs a "buy and hold" philosophy which minimizes portfolio turnover which keeps expenses down. This also lowers tax expense because of less frequent trading. Index Funds provide good diversification for a portfolio.

Exchange-Traded Funds (ETFs)

ETFs are like other Index Funds, but you don't buy and sell shares from the fund company; they are listed on an exchange. You must have a brokerage account to buy and sell them. You can buy and sell ETFs anytime of the day instead of waiting for the price at the end of the day. Having to pay transaction fees to your broker for buying or selling shares can make a difference in your expenses if you do much trading. Some brokerages offer ETFs trade commission free.

Stop orders, limit orders and short selling are possible with ETFs. ETFs are also tax efficient because they don't require frequent trading, and they have an ability to minimize the capital gains they are required to distribute to shareholders (See your tax accountant for more advice).

MUTUAL FUND ANALYSIS

Points to look for:

- Fund Objective
- Management Experience
- Investment Policy
- Investment Holdings
- Fund Performance
- Fees and Charges
- Portfolio Turnover
- Risk

INDEX FUND ANALYSIS

Points to look for:

• What index does the fund track?
• How closely does the fund replicate the target
  index?
• Fund performance
• Fees and Charges
• Portfolio Turnover
• Risk

Where to look for Information

• The Prospectus of the fund company
• Financial Websites
• Your broker's website
• The SEC website (Edgar)

CONCLUSION

Investing involves risk and reward. The companies you invest in may become less profitable or even go bankrupt. You could lose money. Not investing also involves risk. Without the rewards from returns on your investments, it is very difficult to reach your goals.

In the Preface, one of the questions was "How much return do I need to achieve my goals?" This is a difficult question to answer because numerous considerations are involved in defining financial goals. You must know where you are financially now. You must also estimate what will change as you near retirement and after you reach retirement. Keeping a budget will help, but you also need to anticipate what will change.

If you have not had much experience in investing, you may want to consult a financial advisor even after doing your research. Be sure the financial advisor you choose has good credentials and a good financial education. Look for a CPA or a CFP who is a fiduciary with experience in the type of investments you are considering. A fiduciary is required by law to manage a client's assets for the client's benefit, not for his or her own benefit. Whether you have the investment experience, or you hire an advisor, it is ultimately **your responsibility** for your investment decisions. **You must be in control of your own investments.**

The material in the tables and the material about researching investments should be useful either in making your own investment decisions, or in understanding and determining the appropriateness of proposals made by an investment advisor.

Above all, use common sense, and be sure to understand the investment. Don't make the mistake my colleague made and try to get rich quick. After doing your own research, invest in companies with good track records, which deliver good and useful products or services. Start building a diversified portfolio as soon as possible to meet your goals for the remainder of your life. The material in this book will help you to make good decisions with your investments and to solve the Investment Puzzle of Risk and Reward. During your career and in retirement, monitor your portfolio, follow your investment plan, and enjoy life.

About the Author

Education

Bachelor's Degree in Business Management with a major in Accounting from the University of Maryland, 1977

Certified Internal Auditor Designation, 1985

Master's Degree in Personal Financial Planning, College of Financial Planning, June 2009

Experience

Auditor, CPA firm of Regardie Brooks and Lewis

Accountant, The U. S. Department of Housing and Urban Development

Chief of Non-Appropriated Accounting, Department of the Army, Fort Meade, Maryland

Auditor, Department of Labor

Business Chair, Advanced Technology Program, National Institute of Standards and Technology

Publications

Self Monitoring Accounting Systems, National Institute of Standards and Technology, U. S. Department of Commerce, March 1995

A Manager's Guide for Monitoring Data Integrity in Financial Systems, National Institute of Standards and Technology, U. S. Department of Commerce, February 1996, Diane Publishing Company, Darby PA, 2001

DISCLAIMER

• I am not associated with any of the companies, products, services, or websites I have mentioned in this book.

• I am not recommending any of the products, investments or investment strategies discussed.

The purpose of this book is strictly educational. The intention is first, to show how risk and reward are related; second, to make you aware of investment costs, taxes and inflation; and third, to suggest ways to research companies for possible investment.

You must decide how to invest, how much risk to take, which investments fit your lifestyle and goals, and which investments are appropriate for your portfolio. You are ultimately responsible for your finances and you must do the work.

ADDITIONAL RESOURCES

Websites

morningstar.com

zacks.com

marketwatch.com

sec.gov/edgar

Publications

Bogle, John C. <u>The Little Book of Common Sense Investing</u>, Hoboken, New Jersey, John Wiley & Sons, Inc., 2007.

Graham, Benjamin, <u>The Intelligent Investor, Rev. Ed,</u> New York, HarperCollins, 1973.

Mayo, Herbert B. <u>Investments an Introduction</u>, The Dryden Press, Harcourt Brace College Publishers, New York, 1993

Sowell, Thomas, <u>Basic Economics</u>, Basic Books, A Member of the Perseus Books Group, Philadelphia, 2015.

BIBLIOGRAPHY

Beginners' Guide to Financial Statement (sic) (2007)
Retrieved from http://www.sec.gov

The Market Returns in Tables 7 through 11 are actual
U. S. Market Data from *Damodaran Online*, Aswath
Damodaran, Professor of Finance, Stern School of
Business, New York University, January 2021

Internal Revenue Service (IRS) Topic No. 404
Dividends (Updated 12-Mar-2021)

IRS Topic No. 409 Capital Gains and Losses from
the IRS (last Reviewed or Updated 12-Mar-2021)

IRS Interactive Tax Assistant - Frequently Asked
Questions (Updated 4-Jan-2021)